Original title:
Trailing Ivy Tales

Copyright © 2025 Creative Arts Management OÜ
All rights reserved.

Author: Lorenzo Barrett
ISBN HARDBACK: 978-1-80581-926-4
ISBN PAPERBACK: 978-1-80581-453-5
ISBN EBOOK: 978-1-80581-926-4

Echoing Leaves in the Quiet Grotto

In the corners where whispers play,
Leaves joke softly, turning gray.
A squirrel dressed up for morning tea,
Serves acorns with a hint of glee.

Beneath the boughs, a frog sings loud,
Wearing a crown, feeling proud.
The trees giggle, barely shake,
As squirrels dance on the old oak's brake.

A raccoon hosts a masquerade,
Where shadows twirl in leafy shade.
All the creatures laugh and prance,
In nature's whimsical, wild dance.

When nightfall drapes the greens in gray,
Mice recite poems, cheeky and sway.
The moonlight's glow can't help but tease,
As shadows waltz with ev'ning breeze.

Lush Memories in Green Twists

In the garden where laughter grew,
Green fingers danced, oh how they flew!
Petunias giggled at daffodil jokes,
While marigolds rolled like silly folks.

The daisies wore hats, the sunflowers boots,
Mischief abounded in flowered suits.
Yet every morning, they'd bloom with style,
Creating memories that made us smile.

The Tapestry of Clinging Life

Vines wrapped secrets around the trees,
Whispered tales carried by the breeze.
A squirrel joked with an owl so wise,
While the butterflies winked with surprise.

Every leaf held a story to tell,
Of climbing adventures and soft-shelled shells.
Each twist and turn in nature's embrace,
Brought laughter and joy to this green space.

Tales Planted in Rich Soil

Seeds of laughter buried down low,
Watered with giggles, watch them grow!
Carrots pretending to be little spies,
While cucumbers wore glasses, oh what a guise!

Radishes blushed underneath the ground,
As peas joined in a merry round.
In this patch where fun never ends,
Nature's jesters, our leafy friends.

A Dance of Time in the Twirling Green

The vines waltzed in a garden so wide,
Chasing shadows with joy and pride.
Each twist of the stem was a goofy turn,
In the playful day, we all would learn.

With every breeze, the leaves would cheer,
As insects joined the rhythm, dear!
A merry jig in the golden light,
Nature's dance, a pure delight!

Threads of Verdant Memory

In gardens where the shadows play,
A tale of leaves and laughter stays.
The vines they twist, they writhe, they spin,
Reminding us where tales begin.

A squirrel sipped on yesterday's dew,
While wise old toads shared secrets too.
A dancing bug, oh what a sight!
Said, 'Last night's feast was quite a bite.'

Stories Woven in Climbing Roots

Upon the fence, a story grew,
Of ants in hats and a slippery shoe.
They danced around in a silly show,
While the wind chimed in with a gentle blow.

The roots beneath spun threads so bright,
Of missing socks that took to flight.
The flowers giggled in colors bold,
As tales of mischief began to unfold.

The Language of Ivy and Time

Whispers wrap in verdant embrace,
An ivy vine painted with grace.
'Could you hear the chatter of bees?'
'They're plotting vacations,' said one with ease.

The ivy chuckled, a green, leafy sage,
'We'll book a trip, a wild adventure stage!'
Each tendril twirled in joyful glee,
As the moon winked down on their jubilee.

Murmurs of the Green Cloak

Under the cloak of emerald hue,
A raccoon juggled with gooey stew.
The laughter echoed through the trees,
As critters joined in with a raspy wheeze.

A frog in a bow tie, so dapper and spry,
Told stories of clouds that scuttled by.
With every croak and chuckle loud,
They celebrated life beneath the shroud.

Whispers of the Vine-Covered Walls

The walls are giggling, can you hear?
A tale of a snail who brought us cheer.
He wore a top hat, quite a fine sight,
Dancing with shadows, beneath the moonlight.

The bricks all chuckle, the ivy sways,
As ants perform dramas in funny ways.
They march in a line, quite a parade,
While the chubby old frog plays serenade.

Between the Leaves and the Stars

In the garden's embrace, the stars peek through,
A raccoon in pajamas gives us a view.
He juggles the apples, oh what a feat,
While the owls applaud, tapping their feet.

There's a cat on a branch, with dreams quite tall,
He thinks he's a lion, king of it all.
But the squirrels just giggle, they know the show,
After all, he's just fluff, not the bravest bro.

Climbing Stories of the Earth

Beneath every leaf lies a tale so grand,
Of a worm with a flag, in this wiggly land.
He hosted a party, oh such a delight,
Dancing 'round roots till the dawn's first light.

The daisies were judges, with crowns on their heads,
While crickets played music from old garden sheds.
Even a turtle joined in with a grin,
He took off his shell to let the fun in.

The Search for the Emerald Secret

In a patch of green, where secrets reside,
A rabbit in goggles took us for a ride.
He showed us the treasures hidden from view,
Like rocks that looked tasty and stones that were blue.

With whispers of wonders, the hedgehogs all cheer,
As they scavenge for snacks, then disappear.
But one crafty fox, with mischievous glee,
Said, 'The real secret? Come follow me!'

Beneath the Canopy of Memory

In the forest where whispers play,
Squirrels trade jokes in a funny way.
A owl hoots at a duck on a spree,
Telling tall tales, oh what a glee!

Branches twist, like a dance of old,
Mice gather round, their stories bold.
The wind chuckles through leaves so bright,
As shadows waltz in the pale moonlight.

Legends of the Verdant Whisper

Underneath blooms of emerald hue,
A rabbit in spectacles peers at you.
He grins and says, 'What's the latest buzz?'
While mushrooms giggle as if they were was.

A snail with a hat takes a slow, sly glance,
At frogs who are plotting a curious dance.
With each leap, they land like a slippery charm,
Tickling the toad who's raised quite the alarm.

Echoes of Nature's Embrace

Laughter echoes through hollowed trees,
As crickets beat drums with carefree ease.
A raccoon juggles with acorns galore,
While the fox rolls his eyes and snorts with a roar.

Up in the sky, a bird starts to sing,
Telling secrets of fantastical things.
Each leaf in the breeze seems to share,
A joke about foxes and their funny hair.

The Enchanted Climb of Solitude

Climbing the ivy, so green and spry,
A lizard wears glasses, oh me, oh my!
He says, "Careful now, this climb is a test,
Don't fall for the humor – we're trying our best!"

A gopher peeks out with a toothy grin,
"Join me for tales of the yarns I spin!"
As the sun sets low, they share a big laugh,
In nature's embrace, no need for a path.

Chronicles Wrapped in Green Shadows

In the garden, laughter grows,
With plants that tickle toes.
Giggling leaves, a leafy parade,
In this green fortress, whims are made.

Silly vines that dance and twine,
Whisper tales of sun and wine.
Squirrels wearing tiny hats,
Planning parties, now imagine that!

A wandering breeze plays a prank,
On sleepy flowers, 'til they sank.
The sun winks, and the shadows sway,
As mischief scripts the perfect day.

In the twilight's warm embrace,
Watch the moonlight join the race.
Each twirl and twist, a silly show,
In green shadows, laughter flows.

Lyrical Ladders of Resilience

Climbing vines with stories bold,
Whisper secrets yet untold.
Hiccups from the grinning flora,
A riddle wrapped in sweet euphoria.

Jokes exchanged with buzzing bees,
As they dance upon the breeze.
Rooted deep with towering glee,
Each twist and turn is pure esprit.

A flower's wink, a leaf's sly grin,
Every day, let the fun begin!
With laughter echoing through the green,
The silliest tales are always seen.

So take this path, let's not delay,
In green alcoves, let's laugh and play.
For every fall, there's joy to gain,
In these lyrical heights, we're never plain.

The Song of Twined Roots

Roots entwined, a musical thrill,
Humming gently up the hill.
Each leaf a note, each stem a rhyme,
Weaving tunes through space and time.

Swinging branches, make a scene,
Silly sprites in shades of green.
With a chuckle 'neath the moon,
The night blooms, a lively tune.

As crickets chirp their nighttime jest,
The branches sway, a playful quest.
A tangle of laughter fills the air,
In this orchestra of greenery, we share.

So sing along with nature's choir,
In every giggle, let's aspire.
For in the roots that twist and sway,
A song of life is here to stay.

Journeys Through a Gilded Canopy

Beneath the leaves, we plot our course,
With critters leading, full of force.
A canopy of gleeful sights,
Where the daylight dances, and the evening bites.

The squirrels tell tall tales of nuts,
As butterflies join in, doing struts.
Every branch, a brand-new ride,
In the merry woods, we take pride.

With laughter bubbling in each glade,
And echoes of joy that never fade.
A path adorned in colors bright,
Adventure's whisper fills our night.

So take a leap to where we roam,
In this lush land, we're far from home.
With each step, mischief leads the way,
In golden lights, we'll laugh and play.

The Heartbeat of Climbing Flora

In a garden where whispers try to climb,
The plants gossip softly, keeping time.
A creeping vine tickles a worn-out chair,
While daisies chuckle at the wobbly air.

The sunbeams dance on leaves so green,
As peas in pods form a raucous scene.
With every twist, the tendrils twine,
Go out for a stroll; it's simply divine.

But oh, that fern with its sneaky prongs,
Laughs at the snail to whom it belongs.
"If I were as slow as you, dear mate,
I'd miss all the fun and delicious plate!"

So let's raise a toast to greens that play,
In this leafy world, we join the fray.
With roots in laughter, we take a chance,
Join nature's humor in a sunny dance.

Mysteries in the Leafy Labyrinth

Through tangled paths where shadows creep,
The ivy whispers secrets, quite deep.
A caterpillar dons a top hat with glee,
Saying, "Hey, did you notice me?"

The hedgehogs chuckle as they pass by,
Wading through fog with a little sigh.
"Why's the rose looking so very coy?
It's hiding its blush, oh, what a ploy!"

In this maze of greens, laughter blooms,
While mushrooms giggle in their soft rooms.
A riddle is told by the bashful bark,
Of a cheeky squirrel and its bold lark.

So wander the lanes, let laughter in,
Where leafy thrills are cheeky and thin.
With every turn, a quirky treat,
In the wild embrace of nature's heartbeat.

Threads of Growth and Grace

A witty little sprout with a curious grin,
Gets tangled in threads of where to begin.
"Am I a flower or just a green weed,
With dreams of blooming and thoughts to feed?"

Butterflies banter, flitting around,
As petals share tales of what's to be found.
"Did you hear what the daffodil did?
It danced with the breeze, oh sir, what a bid!"

Roots rumble laughter beneath the ground,
In this network of joys where capers abound.
"A tangled affair, may I join in a jest,
For growing together, I think is the best!"

So let's weave our stories, a colorful lace,
In the garden of life, full of humor and grace.
With each little sprout, we'll spark a delight,
In this patch of laughter, both day and night.

Whims of the Wandering Vines

A vine with a whimsy, so sprightly and bold,
Whispers to hedges secrets untold.
"The wind is my partner in this frolic dance,
Let us sway together, oh take a chance!"

The tulips gasp at a roguish chime,
As tendrils twirl in perfect time.
"Why be formal when we can sway?
Life's too short for a dull bouquet!"

A fence post giggles, having its say,
"Why not bloom wildly? Come join the play!"
With leaves that tickle and blooms that mock,
Their laughter tickles the old garden clock.

So follow the paths where whimsies unwind,
In this verdant swath, fun you will find.
With each twist and turn, let the laughter thrive,
In the joyous embrace of the wandering vine.

The Legendary Trails of Green Thickets

In the thicket where tales grow,
Mice hold conferences, don't you know?
With cheese as currency, laughs in the air,
A wise old owl is quite the debonair.

Squirrels in jackets, looking quite grand,
Debate on the best nut in the land.
The hedgehogs giggle, rolling in glee,
While the rabbits do yoga to stay stress-free.

Frogs croak ballads from sunlit rocks,
As mushrooms dance and time paradox.
Each leaf a whisper, a chuckle we hear,
In the thickets where dreams twine with cheer.

With the sun setting low, tales never end,
In this realm of laughter, all hearts mend.
Nature's jesters, with charm and with sass,
In green thickets giggle as moments pass.

Harmony in Twining Threads

Vines braid stories in a tangled mess,
While gnarly roots gossip, never less.
Crickets chirp songs only plants understand,
As dandelions bloom in a fairytale band.

A clever chameleon jests with his hue,
"You can't catch me, I'm clever, it's true!"
Butterflies giggle at a stubborn old snail,
While a crow tells jokes from a lofty trail.

The daisies debate about sun vs. shade,
In the dance of seasons, memories are made.
Each twine a tale, full of jest and delight,
As the night holds laughter and stars shining bright.

In gardens alive with whimsy and glee,
Laughter grows wild, as wild as can be.
Nature's own clowns, in a riotous dress,
Twine threads of joy in comical excess.

Journey Into the Woven Wilderness

In a forest where vines weave a nest,
Woodland creatures gather for a quest.
With acorns as maps, they hop and they wave,
Branding themselves as the brave and the brave.

Raccoons in masks, thieves of the night,
Stealing the snacks from the squirrels with might.
Old owls tell stories, both silly and wise,
While butterflies giggle and roll their eyes.

Every twig a pathway, each leaf holds a jest,
They dance through the brambles, it's truly the best.
A glimpse of a fox playing hide and seek,
Just wait, he says, till I show you my peak!

In this woven world, laughter takes flight,
As the sun brings a glow, and the moon bids goodnight.
With each twist and turn, a chuckle to share,
Journey through laughter, the wilderness flair.

Stones and Leaves in Harmony

Upon the stones, the leaves take their stand,
A silly debate on who's softer, so grand.
"I rustle!" says leaf, with a flutter and roll,
Stones just chuckle, they have their own goal.

Bumbles and giggles from moss-covered rocks,
As beetles play tag, dodging dirty socks.
A quirk of a worm with jokes to unfurl,
Tickles the ground in a whimsical whirl.

A jolly old tree leans close with a grin,
"In the dance of the seasons, we all win!"
For every great boulder that can't help but tease,
There's a leaf that responds with a twirl in the breeze.

From the smallest pebble to the grand tallest oak,
Each one contributing to nature's soft poke.
In stones and leaves, laughter finds its way,
A humorous ballet, come shine or come gray.

Chronicles Beneath the Emerald Veil

In gardens where the green things creep,
The ivy laughs as it starts to leap.
It tickles toes and clings to shoes,
A mischievous prank—what a ruse!

The fence it climbs without a care,
A green magician with skill to spare.
It dances shadows in the sun,
A jester's trick, oh, what fun!

Branches sway, an ivy ball,
Gossiping leaves in a leafy hall.
They whisper secrets in the breeze,
"Oh, look at us! We're experts at tease!"

With every twist, a tale unfolds,
Adventures scribed in leafy folds.
A cozy stage for lizards to play,
Oh, how the ivy loves a showy display!

Tangles of Green and Memory

Once I tripped on a vine so bold,
It told a story of days of old.
With laughter echoing in the space,
It wrapped around my hapless waist.

A little bird perched up high,
Said, 'Are you stuck? Give it a try!'
I laughed and swayed, a green cocoon,
Guess dancing with ivy became my tune.

Memories swirl like petals in air,
Each twist a giggle, each turn a dare.
They whisper loudly, 'Don't you recall?'
That time you tangled with the garden wall!

With roots and leaves, a playful spree,
Every inch reveals an Ivy glee.
So here's to the mischief that grows in sight,
In tangles of green, we find delight!

The Roots of Lost Time

Time's roots are sneaky, they wriggle and twist,
The ivy chuckles, 'You can't resist!'
It pulls you back to moments gone,
Where socks went missing and laughs were drawn.

In a time-warp zone, things start to fray,
Ivy's caught puzzles at play all day.
A leaf like a calendar in disguise,
Marking the days that leave us surprised.

It whispers softly of wishes and dreams,
Of potions brewed from sunlight beams.
In every nook, time giggles wide,
Lost in ivy, it takes you for a ride!

If you pause and listen, you might just find,
A comical tale intertwined, unconfined.
With roots so silly, you trip on a rhyme,
In the garden of laughter, we dance through time!

Nature's Whisper Between the Stones

Between the stones, the ivy creaks,
A comedy act in nature speaks.
It wiggles and writhes, a lively sprite,
Turning the mundane into delight.

"Oh dear!" it sighs with a leafy grin,
"Pardon my dance, I'm here to win!"
As it pockets pebbles and sways in glee,
Nature's tough giggler, oh can't you see?

A playful plot, a jumbled mess,
With roots like fingers, it strives to impress.
It often trips on its own green feet,
Poking at daisies with a cheeky beat.

From cracks in the wall, it seizes its chance,
A show of wild antics, a leafy dance.
So join in the laughter, don't hold back the cheer,
For nature's whispers are meant to endear!

The Language of Arched Canopies

Under leafy whispers, secrets dance,
A squirrel's chatter, a playful prance.
Beneath the boughs, we hide and peep,
While giggles echo, and mischief creeps.

Draped in green, we play charades,
With nature's joy, our laughter invades.
Checkered light falls like buttered toast,
We're hiding here, but we love to boast.

A bird sings jokes, a silly tune,
Buzzing with joy, like a playful balloon.
The sun pokes through, a flickering tease,
Together we tumble with giggling ease.

In this leafy world where shadows play,
Life is a joke, come laugh and stay.
Each rustling leaf holds a funny thing,
In the arched canopies, we toast and sing.

Climbing Shadows and Sunlight

Oh, the shadows wiggle with glee,
As the sunlight tickles every tree.
Climbing high is a game we know,
Jumping from branch to where winds blow.

The sun's a jester, lighting the ground,
While shadows play hide and seek all around.
I trip over roots with a gleeful shout,
Dancing away, what's it all about?

Through patches of warmth, we bounce and glide,
With whispers of laughter, shadows collide.
Roots tell stories of mischief past,
Each twist and turn, a fun contrast.

Chasing the light as it ebbs and flows,
With every ripple, my silly heart grows.
Here in this theater, we play and prance,
In the sunlight's embrace, we seize the chance.

Echoes of Nature's Threads

In the fabric of green, giggles spin,
Like threads in the wind, where laughter begins.
Nature's own tapestries, woven with cheer,
Create funny echoes for all who can hear.

A butterfly flutters, a prankster at heart,
Painting the air like natural art.
Grocery bags clatter, a raccoon in disguise,
All in this garden of whispers and sighs.

Dew-drops glisten like disco balls,
While distant crows croon out spirited calls.
The trees chuckle under their leafy crowns,
As life scampers past in whimsical towns.

Every twist, every turn, a giggling embrace,
In the tapestries spun, we find our place.
Nature's threads form a comic delight,
In these echoes of wonder, we bask in the light.

The Story Inside the Green Enclosure

Behind the vines, a tale unfolds,
Of mischief and jest that never grows old.
Enter the green, a playground of bliss,
Where each corner hides a giggling twist.

Lizards gossip, they're the neighborhood spies,
While squirrels plot under soft, clouded skies.
With jesters and clowns, all here on display,
Watch as the world laughs its worries away.

Frogs croak ballads with buggy eyes wide,
They bring the audience, full of pride.
Every leaf a chapter, every branch a scene,
In this green enclosure, laughter reigns supreme.

So let's tell tales of silly shenanigans,
Of playful jesters and their silly pan-ans.
Under the arch, we'll giggle and play,
In the story we craft, come join our array!

The Green Embrace of Forgotten Lore

In the garden of whimsy, secrets play,
Where shadows dance and giggle all day.
A turtle in trousers, oh what a sight,
Claims he's the king of the garden, alright!

Each vine has a story, a snippet of jest,
Of frogs in top hats who never take rest.
They waltz with the daisies, they jive with the sun,
And plot silly pranks, oh what joy and fun!

A snail with a monocle leads the parade,
While ants in a conga line serenade.
With each bend of ivy, a chuckle unfolds,
Nature's grand theater, a joy to behold!

So tiptoe through greens, where laughter unpacks,
In tales of the wild, where tickles relax.
The whispers of foliage, a sweet little tease,
Unraveling lore with the softest of breeze.

The Tales that Flew with the Vines

From curl to twirl, let's forget our woes,
The vines weave a tale as the sun gently glows.
Where ladybugs gossip and butterflies prance,
Each leaf holds a story, each stem a chance!

Wandering squirrels in a wild debate,
Can acorns be hats, or must they wait?
With laughter like bubbles, they rise to the sky,
In a leafy symposium, oh my, oh my!

A wise old crow caws wisdom and cheer,
Says, "Follow the vines, adventure is near!"
The dandelions giggle as they spin about,
In this vine-draped world, there's never a doubt.

So come take a stroll where the silliness grows,
With tales of the vines, let your laughter flow.
Join the merry creatures, the folly, the fun,
In the garden of giggles, we all are as one!

Hidden Journeys in Leafy Labyrinths

In a maze made of green, whimsy lies thick,
With paths full of giggles, come take your pick.
A toad with a top hat leads all the stray,
Through secrets and laughter, where follies hold sway.

A hedgehog named Henry plays peek-a-boo,
With flowers that tickle, as soft as a shoe.
They snicker and chortle with each little turn,
For hidden adventures await there to learn.

Underneath tangled vines, squirrels compose,
An opera of nuts - just look at their pose!
With choruses bubble and melodies bright,
In this leafy labyrinth, everything's light.

So journey and wander through laughter-wrapped bends,
In nature's own riddle, where joy has no ends.
Each leaf rustles secrets, each shadow a jest,
In hidden green realms, there's fun to ingest!

Secrets of the Nature's Silhouette

Under the shade of the leafy delight,
Whispers of nature echo day and night.
A raccoon with style, in shades so grand,
Hides mischief in pockets, oh isn't it grand?

The shadows giggle, the flowers all grin,
As clovers huddle close, a good joke to spin.
In a world turned upside down moments they chase,
While dandelion puffs float with grace.

An orchestra of chirps, a symphony bright,
With winks from the willows, a wonderful sight.
As leaves swish and sway, with tales to unfold,
In the secrets of twilight, adventure is sold.

So dance through the dusk, with silliness near,
Embrace all the quirks that the woodland holds dear.
For in nature's silhouette, fun's your best friend,
Where every twig bends to laughter, they'll lend!

Whispers Among the Vines

In the garden, vines entwine,
A squirrel wearing a tiny hat,
Whispers secrets that are divine,
While pretending to chat with a cat.

Bamboo straws serve as tiny pipes,
Sipping dew on a sunny morn,
The flowers giggle, sharing gripes,
As the lazy bee smiles, still unborn.

A lizard struts with feigned poise,
Declaring he's the king of flies,
Yet all the bugs make too much noise,
They laugh while tossing him surprise pies!

Underneath the leafy shade,
A thyme fairy finds her lost ring,
But the mischievous bugs invade,
And join her dance with a zing!

Shadows of Green Dreams

In the twilight, shadows play,
A raccoon juggles acorns bright,
While cheeky frogs hop in the fray,
Underneath the moons' soft light.

Caterpillars wear tuxedos,
Swaying to a funky beat,
While spiders spin disco 'neos,
At the party of the street.

Beneath the leaves where secrets hide,
A turtle tells tall, silly tales,
Of how he once managed to glide,
On a breeze with staff of gales!

Mushrooms pop like party hats,
Each claiming they've won the race,
But in reality, it's just chats,
Among the leaves, a friendly space.

Secrets in the Leafy Aisles

In leafy aisles, whispers bloom,
A snail dons sunglasses with flair,
As the beetle plays a bassoon,
Creating music that fills the air.

A shy fern tells a joke or two,
While ants pass by with tiny snacks,
Their laughter echoes, crisp and new,
As grasshoppers plan their attack!

Underneath the twinkling stars,
A fox unveils a stunt untold,
Soaring with the grace of Mars,
As the owls watch, not too bold.

Vines entwined like brothers' arms,
Twist and twirl in a dance so merry,
While the hedgehog struts his charms,
Dressing up in wild berry!

Embrace of the Climbing Spirits

In a world of climbing sprites,
A butterfly winks as he flies,
With witty puns and silly bites,
While the daisies roll their eyes.

The willow shakes its long, green hair,
To the rhythm of a light breeze,
While the bumblebee brushes the air,
Guiding a troupe of giggling leaves.

A raccoon's cooking in the breeze,
Whipping up a stew of glee,
With vines all tangled like they tease,
Making shadows dance for free!

When moonlight spills on the ground,
Laughter echoes, both loud and sweet,
With a garden party all around,
As even the weeds tap their feet.

Legends Among the Stems

In the garden, plants conspire,
To tell tales of a plucky flyer.
A gnome with socks pulled high and bright,
Rides a snail in the moon's soft light.

Flowers giggle, twirling in glee,
While the grasshoppers sing in harmony.
The beetles dance, their shells a-shine,
As clouds above seem to sip on wine.

A squirrel plots to steal a treat,
Wearing a hat, oh, isn't he fleet?
With acorns tucked beneath his chin,
He swears it's the best he's ever been.

Leaves rustle, secrets they share,
Of mischief done with utmost flair.
The legend grows with every twist,
Of gardens where the silly exist.

The Heart of the Hidden Garden

In the shade where shadows play,
A cactus wears a sunhat, they say.
With a grin and spines that glow,
It welcomes friends, both high and low.

Ladybugs giggle on a leaf,
Telling tales, oh, what a relief!
While rabbits wear their Sunday best,
Competing in a hopping contest.

A butterfly flaunts wings so grand,
Challenging the ants to a dance band.
With a flutter and a cheeky wink,
They spin around, pouring lemonade to drink.

In this garden, socks mismatched,
Plants and critters, happily hatched.
With laughter echoing, they unite,
In secrets well-kept, hidden from sight.

The Veil of Verdant Whispers

Under leaves where secrets dwell,
A whisper floats, a ringing bell.
A lizard claims he's a dragon, bold,
While the frogs croak tales from ages old.

An owl in glasses reads a book,
Teaching squirrels, just take a look.
With every page, hysterical sights,
They ponder physics on starry nights.

The vines weave gossip, tangled and wild,
As a curious worm plays the part of a child.
With every giggle, a petal doth sway,
Creating laughter that brightens the day.

The air is thick with fun and glee,
As flowers sway, setting the scene free.
In this joyful realm so lush,
Every bump in the garden stirs a blush.

Secrets Entwined in Green

Between the leaves, stories collide,
As mint sprigs overlap with pride.
A catnap under a fern's embrace,
Gives the dew drop a softer place.

A tortoise in shades, oh, so wise,
Claims he's after the biggest prize.
A cookie jar full of gummy bears,
But those are just the garden's snares.

Petunias gossip about the breeze,
As jumpy weeds spin tales with ease.
Mice in bow ties offer a treat,
While daisies resist the urge to tweet.

In this laughter-laden, leafy world,
Where every secret's wildly unfurled,
Nature's mysteries, oh, what a sight,
In the garden's embrace, all feels just right.

Climbing Towards Forgotten Horizons

In the garden where the shadows play,
A vine thought it could swing all day.
It clambered high with a curious grin,
But tangled up where the fun began.

A squirrel joined in with acrobatic flair,
Challenging the ivy to a daring dare.
"Bet you can't reach that old bird's nest!"
The vine replied, "I'm feeling blessed!"

They climbed and slipped, a comical sight,
Chasing each other from left to right.
With each little leap, the ivy took flight,
Spinning tall tales amid the moonlight.

Though both fell down in a heap of glee,
They laughed so loud the flowers agreed.
For up above, the stars would twinkle,
Cheering on their giggles and every wrinkle.

Echoes of Ivy's Embrace

In a garden nook where whispers bloom,
A vine found joy in chasing gloom.
"Why say goodbye? Let's play instead!"
It wrapped 'round trees like a comfy bed.

A bird chuckled, "What a tangled mess!
You think you're funny? I must confess.
With every loop and every twist,
You've got my tail in a funny tryst!"

They danced around in a clumsy whirl,
While butterflies giggled at every twirl.
"What a pair of goofballs we've become,
With flowers laughing, we're never glum!"

The sun beamed down on their leafy spree,
While snickers rang out from every tree.
Echoes of laughter would soon take flight,
As nature chuckled through day and night.

The Journey Beyond the Garden Wall

A curious vine once dreamed so wide,
To leap beyond where the flowers bide.
With each little tug, it declared, "I'll roam!
Adventure awaits beyond this dome!"

But as it stretched, it caught a fence,
"Is this the end? It feels intense!"
A nearby bee buzzed with frank delight,
"Just ask for help, it's worth the fight!"

So, off it went with a bouncy cheer,
But tangled up in a matted smear.
"Why's this wall such a chubby foe?
I guess I'll climb a bit slower, you know?"

Yet every poke and prick in the air,
Made it giggle loud with vibrant flair.
For every fall brought a giddy chuckle,
The journey was worth every little buckle.

Ascent of the Verdant Soul

A vine once claimed it could touch the sky,
With leafy whims and a daring spy.
It wrapped around trunks and clambered high,
Yelling, "I'll be the next bird to fly!"

But as it climbed, it got stuck real tight,
"Help me, dear critters, it's quite a plight!"
A snail crept by with a careful gaze,
"Adventure called, now you're in a maze!"

They giggled together in leafy disguise,
As squirrels stood proud with twinkle-eyed lies.
"Onward and upward, let's make it grand!
Life's more fun when you have a band!"

At last, released, they danced with cheer,
The journey combined, they held each dear.
For what is life but a silly climb,
With laughter and friends, it's always prime!

Notes from the Green Overpass

On the wall, the green leaves sway,
Whispering secrets, come what may.
They tickle the pigeons, make them dance,
Mischief in sunlight, a vine-filled romance.

One day a squirrel might just take a ride,
On a leafy rollercoaster, oh what a glide!
With acorn helmets and brave little paws,
They zip through the leaves, a crowd goes 'Wow!'

The ivy giggles, it knows the tricks,
It pulls pranks on humans with leafy flicks.
"Hey, watch where you're going!" the vines seem to shout,

As they steal your lunch, without any doubt.

So if you see greens with a chuckle or two,
Remember the mischief that they love to do.
Take care on that path, look up and beware,
For the green overpass holds tales beyond compare.

The Parable of the Climbing Green

In the garden, a sneaky green creep,
Claims the fence like it's a dream so deep.
It climbs up high, and it waves to the sun,
While the daisies below say, "This isn't fun!"

A ladybug gets caught in the fray,
"Help me!" it shouts, in a hilarious way.
The vines start to giggle as they wind and twirl,
They love holding parties, what a wild whirl!

They share a good laugh with the beetles so proud,
In a leafy hideout, away from the crowd.
"We'll teach them to climb!" the brave sprouts all cheer,
As they pull up the daisies with giggles and sneers.

And thus the lesson of vines is loud and clear,
Not all climb with grace, some just persevere.
Laughter and vines make a curious team,
In the tales of the garden, where the wild things dream.

The Tapestry of Pierre and Vine

Once a fellow named Pierre wore a garland of green,
With vines intertwined, quite the lovely scene.
He swaggered with flair, a true leafy king,
Until nature sent fog, which made the birds sing.

The vines thought it funny, a real laugh-out-loud,
As Pierre stumbled forward, head high and proud.
He tugged on a branch, and oh what a sight,
The vines wrapped around, in a wild leafy fight!

"I'm stuck!" cried poor Pierre, as he twirled round and round,
With every attempt, he found himself bound.
The birds perched above with a chorus so sweet,
Chortled and laughed at his vine-dancing feat.

But Pierre learned to laugh, he swayed with the leaves,
And twirled through the garden with newfound beliefs.
For who could resist the fun vines bestow?
In the dance of the green, the laughter would grow.

Vines that Tell Stories of Old

In a garden where vines spin tales through the ages,
They weave through the trellis, like wise little sages.
With knots and with twists, they share stories grand,
Of peas that have danced and tomatoes unmanned.

One day a wise vine told a tale so absurd,
Of a snail who dreamed big, flying high like a bird.
"With wings made of leaves, he'd soar like a kite,
But ended up stuck in a night full of fright!"

The daisies burst out in a riotous cheer,
"Oh snail, go for it! Don't let your dreams steer!"
So he climbed through the greens, with a heart so bold,
While the vines kept on laughing, their humor not cold.

With whimsical whispers carried far by the breeze,
The vines kept their secrets, with giggles and tease.
So listen close, as they murmur and sway,
For stories of old bring the sunshine to play.

The Rise of the Emerald Path

In the garden where brambles dance,
The leaves whisper secrets at every chance.
A snail wearing glasses, quite the sight,
Claims he's the king of the leafy night.

Old vines tell stories, a jumbled mess,
Of wandering gnomes in a tiny dress.
They trip on their roots, oh what a sight,
Laughing so hard, they forget the night.

The blooms hold their breath, in giggles they quiver,
As rabbits in bowties make the weeds shiver.
With hats made of daisies, they sashay around,
While the earthworms chuckle beneath the ground.

So come take a stroll where the green things play,
In a tangle of joy, that brightens your day.
The path is alive with whimsy and cheer,
Where laughter grows tall, year after year.

Stories from the Green Veil

Behind the leaves, there's a raucous show,
With ladybugs laughing in topsy-turvy rows.
A caterpillar in shades sips tea on a leaf,
Spinning tall tales that bring such relief.

The petals come together, a gossip-filled crew,
Grapevines whispering wild stories anew.
A llama on roller skates zooms by,
While bees with sunglasses fly high in the sky.

A terracotta pot claims it's wise and grand,
But spills all its dirt on the soft green land.
The herbs roll their eyes, and the thistles just snort,
As they tune in for tales, of an odd little sort.

In this lush theater, where humor does bloom,
Join the giggles and chuckles dispelling all gloom.
With every green moment, merriment grows,
In this vibrant playground where laughter flows.

Lattice of Life's Embrace

Up in the lattice, the spiders conspire,
Weaving their dreams like a fanciful choir.
A cricket who plays the tiniest flute,
Sings tunes for the grass, with a wink and a hoot.

The sunflowers twist with a giggly delight,
Daring each other to dance through the night.
Ants donning top hats march to the beat,
Bringing the party with tiny, proud feet.

Moss-covered wonders slither and slide,
As mushrooms spin tales of an underground ride.
A fox tries to juggle with roots in the air,
But fumbles and tumbles, much to his despair.

In this muddled maze of green and of glee,
Where laughter hangs thick, and the world feels free.
The lattice of life, with its hilarious grace,
Is a tapestry woven, a whimsical place.

Tales Unfurled by the Winds

Whispers of stories fly high on the breeze,
As dandelions dance, and the soft grass teases.
A squirrel in socks shares his nutty routine,
While waving to flowers in shades of bright green.

Butterflies flutter in sparkly attire,
Playing tag with the wind, they spin and they spiral.
A hedgehog in boots rolls right into a pond,
Causing a splash that leaves everyone donned.

The breeze carries laughter, a playful embrace,
While leaves stitch together in a flittering race.
A bear on a tricycle zooms down a lane,
Honking at bees with a giggle and gain.

So take to the fields where the antics unfold,
With mischief and joy in each tale that is told.
For in every corner of nature's embrace,
Lies the promise of laughter, a whimsical space.

Letters Written in Leafy Ink

In the garden where letters grow,
A snail stole my pen, don't you know?
He scribbled a note, but it said,
"I'm tired of roaming, just keep your bread!"

A butterfly danced on a script full of cheer,
While the squirrels debated who'd read it this year.
The hedges played characters, taking their bows,
As frogs croaked the ending, deserving of wow!

But then came the rain, and the ink ran away,
Leaving me messages I couldn't replay.
The trees whispered secrets, so funny and free,
In a world where the leaves told their tales with glee!

Oh, those leafy adventures, so endless and bright,
With chatty green friends who just love to recite.
I'll pen my own story, on petals so soft,
In the garden of giggles, where laughter takes off!

Reverberations from the Climbing World

The vines had a meeting, quite high in the trees,
Where reporters of nature were buzzing like bees.
With laughter, they shared tales of climbing disgrace,
A raccoon who fell, and his stumblings of grace!

"Hey look at me, I'm the king of this wall!"
Cried a vine with a swagger, so proud of it all.
But a gust of wind teased, and down he did go,
A tangle of leaves turned into a show!

"Why do we climb?" asked the flowers one day,
"Is it for the sunshine, or just to relay
Our secrets to birds, who then sing them with glee?"
And the roots shook their heads—"Just pass us the tea!"

So up they go, tangled, twisted, and spry,
While the sunbeams chuckle and wink from the sky.
In a world filled with laughter, where stories entwine,
Each vine's a comedian, oh, life is divine!

Whispers of Climbing Greens

In the forest so lively, the greens have their say,
They whisper of mischief in their leafy ballet.
A chipmunk with gossip took center stage bright,
As he spun tales of vines dancing all night!

"Did you hear 'bout the blossom who tripped on a root?
And landed with style in a pile of cute loot?"
The leaves shook with laughter, the petals turned red,
As they shared all the secrets that nature had bred.

Through branches and twigs, the stories took flight,
Of a lizard who fancied himself quite the sight.
He posed like a model, on a rock by the stream,
But slipped with a splash—oh, what a big dream!

The greens love a good jest, and they thrive on the fun,
For in nature's rich tapestry, joy has begun.
With glimmers of humor that brighten the scene,
The whispers of climbing greens reign supreme!

The Secrets of Vine and Stone

In a garden of wonders where secrets first sprout,
The stones hold old tales, but they laugh out loud!
A vine whispered softly, "Can you keep a beat?"
While chuckling at rocks laid back in the heat.

"I've seen kings and queens at this very spot,
But who needs a crown if you've got a nice lot?"
The stones chuckled deep with a rumbly cheer,
While the vine climbed higher, no worries, no fear!

They laughed at the raindrops that fell from the sky,
With stones soaking in humor as clouds drifted by.
"Let's dance in the puddles!" the vine twirled with glee,
As the whole garden joined in a joyful spree!

So here's to the tales we spin from our heart,
With vine and with stone, we will never part.
In a world filled with laughter, let's keep the fun flowing,

For the secrets of nature are constantly growing!

Tales from the Lush Canopy

A squirrel thought he was a king,
He wore a hat made of string.
A bird laughed, perched on a bough,
"You rule the nuts! But where's your crown?"

The leaves whispered secrets of fun,
As critters danced under the sun.
A raccoon pranced with a shiny prize,
A stolen snack from a surprised fry.

But oh, the trouble that they found,
When ants formed a march all around.
They scurried and carried each crumb away,
Leaving the party in disarray!

In the shade, laughter mixed with play,
What a ruckus in the leafy fray!
Everyone joined in the delightful mess,
Nature's humor—oh, what a jest!

Embracing the Wild Walls

The vines decided they would dance,
To twirl and sway, oh what a chance!
A rabbit hopped, gave a little clap,
As flora began their leafy rap.

A butterfly snickered, wings all aglow,
"Can plants really groove? Let's make it a show!"
The daisies swayed to the beat so sweet,
While bees buzzed along, tapping their feet.

In shadows, a toad joined the throng,
With croaks that sounded like a song.
The garden erupted, a wild display,
With laughter overlapping in a quirky array.

As night drew near, they struck a pose,
A party of greens where no one dozed.
Patch after patch, they chatted and cheered,
Nature's antics—joy never seared!

Chronicles of the Winding Stem

A winding stem told tales galore,
Of potted plants and garden lore.
"One day I reached up to the sky,
But a friendly frog made me cry!"

He laughed at the stem, all twirly and round,
"Watch your head when you're looking down!"
The buds around giggled, swayed in delight,
As the stories flowed into the night.

A gnome popped up in his miniature hat,
"Do I look silly, or just like a brat?"
The flowers replied with petals aglow,
"Just embrace the wild—and put on a show!"

What mischief brewed among the greens,
With vines knitting sweaters—oh, what a scene!
In every twist and every bend,
Nature's chuckles would never end!

The Clench of Nature's Grip

In a tangle of roots, a kitten got stuck,
It mewed in panic, 'Oh, what bad luck!'
A wise old snail, slow yet bright,
Said, "It's a game; we'll set it right!"

With a twist of a vine and a clever flip,
They turned the struggle into a trip.
Soon they were laughing, all mired in mess,
Nature's grip turned into a jest!

A hedgehog snorted, rolling in glee,
"Next time you climb, maybe just ask me!"
They tied up the tales of the ruckus they made,
Nature's humor—never to fade!

So when you're caught in life's silly seed,
Just laugh along; it's the way to succeed.
For in every snare, there's room for a grin,
Let the wild games of life begin!

The Saga of the Green Strands

In the garden, green tendrils creep,
Whispering secrets of vines so deep.
They tickle the walls, a cheeky embrace,
Playing hide and seek, what a silly race.

A squirrel chases, in a wild spree,
Through the leaves, like a giggling bee.
They wiggle and twist, in playful delight,
Nature's comedy show, what a funny sight!

With each little leaf, a giggle is found,
In the jungle gym where squirrels abound.
They somersault down, a clumsy display,
Rolling on laughter, come join the fray!

So let's raise a toast to laugh and cheer,
To the green strands that bring us near.
For while they may cling, with sly little grins,
In their leafy embrace, the joy truly begins!

Shades of Life's Twisting Paths

Along the fence, the green curls sway,
Telling tales of mischief in a playful way.
They peek through cracks, with a wink and a smile,
Promising giggles for just a short while.

Beneath the sun, flexing with glee,
A frolicsome dance, wild and free.
They jive with the wind, what a sight to behold,
Even the old stones can't help but be sold.

At dusk they whisper, secrets they share,
About the neighbors' cat with a wild scare.
Oh, the tales they weave of the days gone past,
In the twists and turns, the fun seems to last!

So come along, take a stroll with me,
Through the paths of laughter, joy's own decree.
In every shadow, in each verdant hitch,
There's humor and joy, and a little bit of stitch!

Legends of the Clinging Heart

There's a tale where the green things cling,
To wooden doors and the joy they bring.
With a bounce and a skip, they cling to the post,
Making every passerby giggle and boast.

With each rusty nail, a story does weave,
Of all the fun days people believe.
They laugh and they chortle, making hearts light,
In the enchanting garden, oh what a sight!

The postman chuckles, the flowers do sway,
Even the busy sun seems to play.
The whispers of green with humorous flair,
Keep the dull moments graciously rare!

So let us toast to the green tales unspun,
To laughter and hugs under the sun.
For in each gentle squeeze, the heart finds its beat,
In legends of green, there's always a treat!

The Veins of Nature's Past

Through the cracks of the walls, vines boldly strut,
They tiptoe along as if in a rut.
Each twist, each turn, a story unfolds,
Of giggly debates and daring molds.

They cradle the stones with a gentle tease,
Singing soft hymns in the rustling breeze.
With a playful nudge and a gentle tug,
Nature's jokes land just like a hug.

As shadows creep in with a sneaky grin,
These green little jesters light up the din.
Their antics narrate the quirks of the day,
In nature's grand circus, come laugh and play!

So here's to the vines and the laughter they bring,
In the tapestry of life, they dance and they sing.
For in every crevice where green things grow,
The humor of nature is sure to flow!

The Labyrinth of Nature's Grip

In gardens where the vines do twist,
A squirrel gets lost in a green mist.
He takes a turn, then stops and stares,
Thinking he's found a spot for wares.

With every branch and turn he makes,
He wonders if it's wine or cakes.
But all he finds is leafy traps,
And ants with schedules and small maps!

The flowers chuckle with a wink,
As our friend ponders, lost in drink.
He'll need a guide, a kind of sage,
To navigate this leafy cage!

At last, he climbs, and climbs so high,
To get a view of the wide sky.
He shouts, "Hey, is there a way out?"
But all he hears is leafy clout!

A Symphony of Climbing Greens

The vines in tune, they twist and sway,
Like dancing friends at a bright soirée.
Each leaf a note, crisp and bright,
Singing songs of day and night.

A snail joins in, with style and grace,
Slides through the party, a lively pace.
He wears a bowtie, proud and neat,
Bobbing along to the leafy beat.

A grasshopper hops, with rhythm so fine,
Chiming in, a jolly good time.
The vines all laugh as they bend and spin,
In this grand concert, where none can win!

And when the sun begins to set,
The orchestra of greens won't forget.
They'll play all night under the moon,
In a leafy symphony, a jazzy tune!

The Spirit of the Climbing Figure

A ghostly figure begins to creep,
Through the garden where secrets sleep.
With ivy tangled in his hair,
He whispers jokes that float on air.

"Why did the lettuce win a race?
Because it ran with a leafy pace!"
The flowers giggle, the vines grow tall,
In this haunting, there's fun for all.

He climbs the trellis with ease and glee,
Planting laughter for all to see.
With each twist and turn, the spirits cheer,
For in laughing joy, there's naught to fear!

As shadows dance and flashlights twinkle,
His jokes unfold, and the mirrors crinkle.
In every knot and twist he finds,
Laughter's bond forever binds!

A Canvas of Leaves and Dreams

On a hill where the colors bloom,
Lives an artist with a wild room.
His brushes dance with nature's hues,
Painting tales of leaves and blues.

A talking leaf falls with a plop,
"Hey there, painter! Don't you stop!"
The painter laughs, grabs that green,
"It's the best model I've ever seen!"

With every stroke, his dreams ignite,
A world where greens come out at night.
Where vines can chat and flowers winks,
And laughter flows in colorful inks.

"Oh, the stories that we could weave,
From leaf to vine, just believe!"
He chuckles loud, paint splattered wide,
In a canvas universe, dreams collide!

Tangles of Time and Treetops

Up high where the sunlight gleams,
A squirrel declares it's time for dreams.
He swings on a branch, oh what a sight,
Chasing the shadows, playing all night.

The winds whisper secrets to leaves of green,
Tickling the branches, a mischievous scene.
A dance of the vines with glee they prance,
Conspiring to join in a leafy romance.

Time tumbles forward, yet here we stand,
Countless giggles in this leafy land.
Atop the world, where laughter rings,
And the silly tales of the forest sing.

So join in the fun, let your laughter flow,
For in treetops high, it's a magical show.
With knots and spirals, let's make our mark,
Life's just a jester when you leap from the park.

The Language of Climbing Hearts

With whispers of laughter, the vines ascend,
Each twist a secret, each curl a friend.
They climb on together, sharing delight,
A union of giggles, dancing all night.

Roots stretch and giggle, they wiggle with glee,
As branches braid together, a sight to see.
A buddy comedy in the dense green shade,
Where every mischief is skillfully laid.

In the language of laughter, they twist and they turn,
Every knot a lesson, every leaf a yearn.
And up in the canopy, heartstrings do play,
As climbing companions, they frolic away.

So raise a cheer, let your spirit be free,
In tangled connections, we find jubilee.
With stories of friendship in each little part,
For with every ascent, we're speaking from the heart.

Stories Woven in Foliage

In the groves of green where the laughter spills,
And the leaves tell secrets, the heart simply thrills.
A quirky old tree shares tales of the past,
As creatures convene for stories to cast.

The branches bobbed like a curious head,
While the squirrels recounted the crumbs they had fed.
Whiskers twitching, the rabbits all lean,
To catch the next joke from the elder unseen.

The moss giggles softly under furry feet,
Mimicking tales from the past, oh so sweet.
In this green theater, the punchlines flow,
With every twist of the vine, the stories grow.

So gather around as we share and we sway,
For nature's a stage in this leafy ballet.
Together we weave through the fables we know,
In stories woven where the wild plants grow.

Dances of the Twisting Tendrils

Under the twilight, the tendrils entwine,
As shadows play tricks in the warm, soft shine.
They giggle and frolic, a whimsical spree,
In a merry jig, just wild and carefree.

The vines spin around like a playful child,
Whispering secrets, in mischief they're wild.
They twist and they turn, always in pairs,
A ballet of buds with nimble affairs.

The moon winks down at the foliage's dance,
As bugs clap their wings in a rhythmic trance.
Roots tap along to an unseen beat,
As the meadow ignites with a jovial heat.

So join in the laughter, let nature unwind,
In the dance of the tendrils, pure joy you'll find.
Each pirouette spun in the soft evening breeze,
Holds the heart and the soul in merry tease.

The Dance of Aerial Tendrils

In the garden, a waltz begins,
Tendrils jiggle with cheeky grins.
They twist and turn, a fanciful play,
Boys and girls, all tangled, hooray!

Laughter echoes through the greens,
As vines do their jig, chasing dreams.
Playful whispers in the breeze,
A dance of joy, with utmost ease.

Watch them spiral, up they climb,
Swaying to a rhythm, oh so sublime.
They haven't a care, nor a reason why,
Just frolicking 'neath the sunny sky.

Join the spree, just take the chance,
Twist your limbs, join the dance.
In the garden, let worries cease,
And join the fun, find your peace.

Growing Together in Silence

Two little vines, side by side,
In silence they grow, with nowhere to hide.
Cracking jokes, but no words are exchanged,
Their laughter in leaves all strangely arranged.

They climb up the wall, without any fuss,
Each twirling tendril whispers, 'Trust us!'
They share a secret, their silent delight,
Under the moon, they giggle at night.

Other plants stare with a puzzled gaze,
'Why don't they chat? How do they blaze?'
But the vines don't mind, they're having a ball,
In silence they grow, together they sprawl.

And when the sun shines, their leaves start to sway,
While passersby chuckle and say,
'Look at those two, growing so near,
In a world of noise, they find laughter here!'

Tales of the Wandering Climber

Once there was a climber, bold and spry,
With dreams to reach the clouds in the sky.
Stumbling and fumbling, he laughed with glee,
'Oh, what fun to climb like me!'

He tickled branches, gave flowers a fright,
Swinging through gardens, a hilarious sight.
Vines followed closely, whispering behind,
'This guy's got style, truly one of a kind!'

He'd trip over stones and dance on the grass,
With a wink and a grin, he'd pass the sass.
Each tale was a riot, laughter would bloom,
As he bounced through the forest, brightening the gloom.

Now those climbing tales are legends so grand,
Of a jovial vine with a clumsy command.
A tale to be shared, time after time,
With giggles and chuckles, it's pure pantomime!

Leaves that Bind Our Stories

In a patch of sun, leaves twirl and sway,
Binding their tales in a whimsical way.
Each one a chapter, a verse or a rhyme,
A tapestry woven through seasons of time.

They gossip of raindrops and giggle at sun,
If leaves could talk, oh what fun they'd run!
Each vibrant hue holds a memory dear,
A story of laughter that's evergreen here.

When the wind whispers, secrets unfold,
Echoes of laughter in colors so bold.
Together they cling, through thick and through thin,
In the book of the garden, smiles never wear thin.

So raise up a toast, to leaves in their spree,
For binding our stories, as sprightly as they be.
In the dance of nature, with joy on display,
Let's celebrate life in this leafy ballet!

Fables in the Foliage's Fold

A snail in a race wore a hat,
He thought he'd outrun a chatty cat.
But the cat just yawned and took a nap,
While the snail got lost beneath a map.

The owl hooted loud with a caw,
He spotted the snail and gave a guffaw.
"In slow motion, you'll win, take a chance!"
The snail sighed deep, "Let's just dance!"

The fern whispered tales of lost socks,
Under leaf cover – oh what a box!
Each plant had a story, a giggle or two,
Of the things they've seen, both old and new.

So remember, dear friend, when you're feeling slow,
Life's hidden in laughter, just watch it flow.
Join the fables in greens where the fun swings,
And don't forget to pack some whimsical things!

Murmurs from the Tangled Trails

In a tangle of vines, a frog found a rhyme,
His croaks turned to songs, oh what a time!
A turtle chimed in with a clumsy beat,
Which made all the bugs get up on their feet.

The rabbits all danced like they had no care,
While a squirrel dropped acorns from way up there.
With each cheerful hop, the branches would sway,
As laughter erupted in wild, leafy play.

A wise old stick bug gave dance lessons too,
"Just wiggle and jive, and you'll feel brand new!"
The crowd all agreed, they were ready to jam,
Even a shy flower joined with a slam!

So if you hear murmurs while out on your walks,
Just maybe it's nature telling you jokes.
Join the fun woodland crew and don't miss the date,
With nature's sweet giggles, you're bound to feel great!

Nature's Silken Scribbles

On a leaf, a spider spun tales out of air,
With threads so fine, they hung with flair.
A ladybug chuckled, her spots all aglow,
"Are you writing a novel? Or just a quick show?"

"A biography!" said the spider with pride,
"Of the squirrels who dash, and the ants who abide.
They mingle and play, they dance in the sun,
While I just sit here, oh how I get spun!"

Down the trail, a raccoon paused to stare,
"What's the secret, dear friend? How do you dare?"
"With patience and whim, and a sprinkle of glee,
I weave every moment, it's all up to me!"

So the next time you wander where wild things stay,
Look for the scribbles in bright green ballet.
Nature writes stories on leaves like a book,
With humor aplenty, come take a look!

Verdant Dreams in the Gloom

In the woods where the shadows and giggles collide,
A gnome named Fred took off on a ride.
He rode on a mushroom, quite high in the air,
While squirrels cheered loudly, "With flair, with flair!"

A bat swooped down, in the twilight so neat,
"Watch out for branches! They'll trip up your feet!"
Fred ducked and he dived, his cap flying high,
As laughter erupted, oh me, oh my!

The fog rolled in thick with a twist and a twirl,
As pixies tossed glitter, making Fred swirl.
They giggled and danced in moonlight's soft beam,
Singing silly songs of a whimsical dream.

So if you find yourself lost in the night,
Keep chasing the giggles and shadows of light.
For amidst verdant dreams where the creatures all loom,
You'll find the best tales in nature's own bloom!

www.ingramcontent.com/pod-product-compliance
Lightning Source LLC
Chambersburg PA
CBHW070315120526
44590CB00017B/2689